Toasts for Life's Occasions

ISBN: 9 781864 7650 6 9

Copyright © Axiom Publishing, 2007.
Unit 2, 1 Union Street, Stepney, South Australia 5069

This book is copyright. Apart from any fair dealing for the purpose of private study, research, criticism or review, as permitted under the Copyright Act, no part may be reproduced by any process without written permission.
Enquiries should be made to the publisher.

AXIOM
AUSTRALIA

www.axiompublishing.com.au

Printed in Malaysia

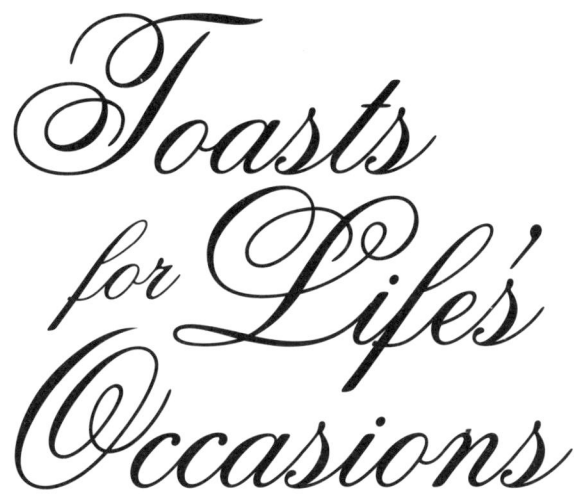

Michelle O'Regan

Contents

Anniversaries 10
    To the couple 11
    From wife to husband 13
    From husband to wife 14
    Special anniversaries 15
Birthdays 17
    General toast 17
    Milestone birthdays 19
Bon voyage 22
Christening/Baptism 25
Christmas 31
Class reunions 35
Easter 38
Eating Blessings in Different Cultural Traditions 40
Family reunions 44
Fathers Day 47
Fellow workers 49
Friendship 50
Graduation 56
Guests 59
Hen's night 61
Historic toasts 63
Hosts and Hostesses 65

House warming	68
Mothers Day	71
"Naughty but Nice" toasts	74
New Years	80
Occupations	86
Recovering from illness	90
Retirement	91
Sports	93
St Patrick's Day	96
Stag's Party	99
Team Won/Lost	102
Valentine's Day	104
Wakes and Remembrances	106
Wassail!–The drinking occasion	108
Weddings	114
To the bride and groom	114
To the groomsmen	117
To the groomsmen	117
To the parents	117
Groom to his bride	118
Bride to his groom	118
Winning the lottery	120

A TOAST FROM THE HOST WITH THE MOST

It's one of those balmy evenings. The conversation flows as easily as wine from the decanter. Cheeks are rosy, belts are straining, good humour abounds. Everyone will go away tonight having enjoyed the occasion immensely, without necessarily remembering too much about the details.

Want to know how to make it memorable? Make a toast, ice the cake of fellowship and good feeling. Climb to your feet, call the unruly table to order, raise your glass, and speak:

> To my dearest friends a toast,
> A few short words from your humble host.
> To friendship, fine wine and a laden table
> And surrender your keys if you don't feel able!

Toasting has been around for about as long as civilization and the shared libation. This social habit of getting together and breaking bread washed down with some fermented brew, made for very convivial gatherings. When all are feeling mellow, the most natural thing in the world is to climb to one's feet and "Wassail! Good health, long life!" to one's companions.

By the 1800s toasts had become a part of the etiquette of celebratory gatherings. A British Duke is reported to have said:

"...Every glass during dinner must be dedicated to someone and to refrain from toasting is sottish and rude, as if no one present was worth drinking to."

Make toasting a part of your life: the garden-variety family get-together, the congenial evening spent with friends or the special celebrations: head-wetting, no longer bed-wetting? Getting hitched, becoming bewitched, another year on the dial, new house, going travelling…

Wherever two or more of you are gathered, seize the day and be prepared with something to say!

So seldom do we voice our appreciation and delight and teasing affection for each other. Delivering a toast is a way to do just that. Enjoy!

TOASTING: THE DO'S AND THE DON'TS

stand when offering a toast unless it's a very informal gathering. Standing grabs the attention of the group. A light tap on the edge of a wine glass should be sufficient in case there's talking (not to be tried on fine crystal!) Face towards the person/s you are toasting.

NEVER stand or drink the toast when it's being directed at you. However, once the toast is offered, stand and respond even if it's just to thank the toast maker

NEVER offer a toast before the host of the evening has had a chance to do so. If this doesn't seem to be on the cards, discreetly ask the host if you could do the honours.

DO NOT push an individual to make a toast when they are not inclined or prepared. You may regret that you did.

NEVER refuse to be part of the toast. Even if you're not drinking alcohol, fill your glass with water or soft drink. An empty glass raised is better than not lifting one at all.

In dining functions where there is a dais, only people on the dais may propose a toast.

Sober enough to toast?

Not sure about your ability to deliver a toast without losing face, or falling flat on it?

If you can pronounce these tongue twisters three times in succession without sounding like a blithering idiot, you're sober enough to make a toast.

Five fuzzy French frogs frolicked through the fields of France.
These sheep shouldn't sleep in a shack;
Sheep should sleep in a shed.

ANNIVERSARIES

"There is nothing nobler or more admirable than when two people who see eye to eye keep house as man and wife, confounding their enemies and delighting their friends."
— Homer, Odyssey, ninth century B.C.

Wedding anniversaries are important for the couple, but more especially for the woman. The man may forget an anniversary but if he does she will never allow him to forget that he forgot for the rest of his natural spousal life. One of the secrets of a happy, peaceful marriage is to remember to mark the occasion with a celebration of some kind.

> A toast to ye married men—
> If you appreciate your wife
> And you really value your life
> Remember the anniversary date
> Plan to treat her, don't hesitate
> Go on, you have lots to celebrate!

Make the occasion special by delivering a memorable toast. Imagine your spouse's delight when you give a heartfelt toast, in front of your family and friends. Or how uplifted the couple will feel when a friend or member of the family make them a toast.

* * * *

TO THE COUPLE

To the secret of long and wedded bliss
Hark ye all and remember this:
Don't dwell on the times when he drove you mad,
Just give her a hug when she's feeling sad,
And remember the good and not the bad!

❋ ❋ ❋ ❋ ❋

The kindest and the happiest pair,
Will find occasion to forbear,
Something, every day they live
Turn a blind eye, and forgive.

❋ ❋ ❋ ❋ ❋

Raise your glasses and offer a toast:
To a loving couple of whom we can boast.
Who've been together for many years,
Through good times and bad, laughter and tears
She still thinks he's handsome, he still makes her swoon
To their life together—one long honeymoon!

❋ ❋ ❋ ❋ ❋

Let's drink a toast to the oldyweds!
Who've been through thick and thin.
They've laughed and cried, toiled and sighed
And every argument he let her…win!

❋ ❋ ❋ ❋ ❋

To Ogden Nash, a remarkable wit, who said:
"To keep your marriage brimming
With love in the loving cup
Whenever you're wrong, admit it;
Whenever you're right, shut up!"

May the life you share
Double the laughter and joy
Halve the troubles and care
On this birthday of your love affair.

※ ※ ※ ※ ※

May there be many more days for you
to grow in each other's affections.

※ ※ ※ ※ ※

May you love each other more than yesterday,
but less than tomorrow.

※ ※ ※ ※ ※

Let anniversaries come and let anniversaries go-
but may your love for each other continue to grow.

※ ※ ※ ※ ※

To the happy pair!
It's nice to see a couple married for so long,
They must be doing something right ---
Or maybe something wrong.

※ ※ ※ ※ ※

To a wise man called Sweeney who said:
"A wedding anniversary is the celebration of love,
Trust, partnership, tolerance and tenacity.
Only the order varies for any given year."

※ ※ ※ ※ ※

Let's toast the recipe to a happy marriage -
That in any argument the husband
Is entitled to the last words
Those words are …(Pause to hear the gasps of outrage from
the women) "Yes dear"

※ ※ ※ ※ ※

All rise and raise a glass,
And toast the loving pair
Who've shown us all in many ways
That love is here to share.

* * * * *

May the wind be always at your back,
The Sun overhead in a clear sky
and the one you love by your side.

* * * * *

Happy marriages begin when we marry the one we love,
and they blossom when we love the one we married.

* * * * *

Here's to true love, may it always be spoken
Here's to true friendship, may it never be broken.

* * * * *

Let's drink a toast to love
A fruit that remains in season throughout our lives!

* * * * *

Let's drink a toast to
The secret of a loving marriage:
Never let the sun go down on an argument
Forgive all slights by nightfall
Wake each day with love in your heart.

FROM WIFE TO HUSBAND

This toast is for you—
We've been married for years
Through good times and bad
You remain the best friend
That I've ever had.

To my darling husband
Who is blind to my faults
And still looks at me
With the same loving gaze
As the day we said, "I do".

✻ ✻ ✻ ✻ ✻

A toast to our happy marriage
Even though we wed many years ago
The celebration continues.
We have never taken for granted
The love we hold for each other.

✻ ✻ ✻ ✻ ✻

Here's to my love, my life, my friend
May our time with each other have no end!

FROM HUSBAND TO WIFE

A toast to my wonderful wife
Who has made for me a home and life.

✻ ✻ ✻ ✻ ✻

To my darling wife
No matter how we fill our days
She's the last person I see each night
And the first smile, soft touch and kind voice
to greet me each morning.

✻ ✻ ✻ ✻ ✻

A toast to my beautiful wife
My debt to you, my love,
Is one I cannot pay
In any coin of any realm
On any reckoning day.

✻ ✻ ✻ ✻ ✻

SPECIAL ANNIVERSARIES

First Anniversary
To my darling wife
Who only a year ago agreed to marry me,
And every day has made me glad
I posed the question on bended knee.

* * * * *

I can't believe a year has passed
Since first you tied the knot
If your marriage was a climate zone
You'd be hot, hot, hot!

* * * * *

Second Anniversary
Two years ago we all assembled
To make your wedding day
And now we celebrate that love
Enduring in every way.

* * * * *

Third Anniversary
Three years have passed since the two of you
Pledged your love one for the other
We hope you both enjoy this day
And each day add another.

* * * * *

Fourth Anniversary
Four years have come and gone
Since first you vowed "I do"
Lift your glasses, drink it down
As we make this toast to the happy two.

* * * * *

Fifth Anniversary
Half a decade and you've passed another mark
What a happy day for all,
Open the champagne, hurry now!
We plan to have a ball!

Tenth Anniversary
For ten years now you've been a pair
You're coming up in aces
Everyone can tell you're still in love
By simply seeing your faces.

Twenty-fifth Anniversary
To a love that has endured!
' twas Mark Twain who said:
No couple knows what perfect love is
Until they have been married at least a
Quarter of a century.

It's your silver anniversary this year
And we just want you to know
Cupid must have been in a great mood the day
When first he shot his arrow.

Fiftieth Anniversary
Fifty years ago, you made a pledge
And promised to be true.
Your family and friends today
Are here in awe of you.
Congratulations!

BIRTHDAYS

It's said the delight we have in our birthdays is inversely proportional to the number we celebrate until…we get over all the midlife angst and are just happy to still be around! If we're fortunate we all get there…to twenty-one, to forty, to fifty, to eighty.

> Let's drink a toast to birthdays,
> They start to accumulate
> But bless the years that you add on
> The alternative's not so great!

A birthday gathering is an excellent opportunity to wish the honoured guest all the best, with maybe a little affectionate teasing thrown in, if that is something they would enjoy or endure. Chances are they'll get their revenge when your birthday comes around.

General Toast

> A toast to having birthdays
> The more you have the longer you live!

* * * * *

> Raise your glass and drink to the reason
> Why all of us have gathered.
> His hair is thinning, his eyesight is bleary
> He goes around calling everyone "Deary!"
> But we love him still and we always will,
> Happy birthday, birthday boy!

* * * * *

To a wonderful woman on her special day
We won't ask you how many that makes.
But take a deep breath and prepare yourself
To blow out candles on several cakes!

✷ ✷ ✷ ✷ ✷

Let's toast another milestone
For the woman of the day
She's been 29 for many a long year
And there she plans to stay!

✷ ✷ ✷ ✷ ✷

If you're worried you're getting older
While the rest of us stand still
We'll all have had a few birthdays
By the time you're over the hill!

✷ ✷ ✷ ✷ ✷

Let's raise our glasses and make a toast
"Happy birthday say us all!"
Enjoy the friends and festivities
We want you to have a ball!

✷ ✷ ✷ ✷ ✷

Let's drink a toast to advancing years.
The older the fiddler, the sweeter the tune!

✷ ✷ ✷ ✷ ✷

A toast to all husbands gathered here
The best way to remember your wife's birthday
Is to forget it once!

✷ ✷ ✷ ✷ ✷

To you on your birthday, glass held on high,
Glad it's you that's older—not I.

✷ ✷ ✷ ✷ ✷

To wish you joy on your birthday
And all the whole year through,
For all the best that life can hold
Is none too good for you.

* * * * *

Let's make a toast to growing older.
May the years in your life run out
Before the life in your years.

* * * * *

Another candle in your cake?
Well, that's no cause to pout,
Be glad that you have strength enough
To blow the damn things out.

* * * * *

Good luck to old age!
May we all get so lucky!

* * * * *

May God grant you many years to live,
for sure he must be knowing,
the earth has angels all too few
and heaven is overflowing...

MILESTONE BIRTHDAYS

Twenty-first birthday
And now you're one and twenty
All sparkling with health and youth
We wish you fortune, love and plenty
And friends who'll speak the truth.

* * * * *

Thirtieth Birthday
Thirty candles on your cake,
'tis getting crowded now
Quick make a wish, as you blow them out
And we all give you a bow!

❅ ❅ ❅ ❅ ❅

Fortieth birthday
Let's toast to turning forty
When all say life begins
Does that mean I'm forgiven
For all my previous sins?

❅ ❅ ❅ ❅ ❅

(And now you stand before us
Mother, friend and wife
We toast you on your special day
And wish you a happy life.)

❅ ❅ ❅ ❅ ❅

Fiftieth Birthday
A toast to the woman who's fifty
My word you're looking fine
Don't worry a bit about the number,
Let me refill your glass of wine!

❅ ❅ ❅ ❅ ❅

We raise our glasses and make a toast
To our much loved birthday guest
With a half a century under his bonnet
And plenty of fuel left in the tank!

❅ ❅ ❅ ❅ ❅

Sixtieth Birthday
Sixty candles on your cake
It'll take a while to light them

And if you need help blowing them out
You have many friends, so invite them!

*****

A toast to mind over matter
If you don't mind about age, then it doesn't matter!

*****

Seventieth Birthday

To a lovely lady of seventy
Whose years have been so full
Your friends and family are gathered here
To wish you many still!

*****

Three score years and ten!
We toast you on this day,
A father, a friend, the best of men
Many returns, hip! Hip! Hooray!

*****

Eightieth Birthday

To be eighty is really something
And lively and loving to boot
You make it look so attractive
We'd like to follow suit!

*****

Ninetieth Birthday

Ninety candles upon your cake!
We drink a toast to you,
The family you have raised and loved
The friends who love you too!

*****

BON VOYAGE

"Bon voyage!" French for "Goodbye! Have a good journey!" Traditionally the bon voyage toast was given when the person or people were travelling afar by sea. These days it is offered to anyone going on holiday or to spend time away, whether they travel by land, sea or air.

Good friends we wish you all the best
On the eve of your going away!
You will be in our hearts; you'll be in our minds
Until you come back to stay.

✳ ✳ ✳ ✳ ✳

May we always part with regret
And meet again with pleasure.

✳ ✳ ✳ ✳ ✳

Here's to you and here's to me
Wherever we may roam,
And here's to the health and happiness
Of the ones we leave at home.

✳ ✳ ✳ ✳ ✳

Happy are we met, happy have we been,
Happy may we part, and happy meet again.

✳ ✳ ✳ ✳ ✳

May the road rise up to meet you
May the wind be always at your back
The sunshine warm upon your fields
And until we meet again
May God hold you in the hollow of his hands.—Irish toast

✳ ✳ ✳ ✳ ✳

Here's to the ones who will soon be gone
May your travels take you far
Here's to the days, the weeks, the months
We'll count until you're home.

* * * * *

To our intrepid travellers
We wish you Bon Voyage!
Hope you've packed your bags
And that nothing nags
"Oh did I switch off the gas?"

* * * * *

To our friends who are leaving
You're going far away
Will you think about us sometimes
'Cos we'll wonder about you every day.

* * * * *

May the patron saint of travellers
Keep you safe from harm
Protect you on your journey
Until once more you're home!

* * * * *

We toast you on your travels;
Though you go far away
And hope you'll come back safe to us
We'll celebrate again that day!

* * * * *

May wherever you hang your hat
Have a door and a welcome mat!

* * * * *

God speed on your journey
And a very fine holiday!

May you unwind and relax
Enjoy your time away.

❊ ❊ ❊ ❊ ❊

Over the sea you go
For months, maybe even years
Carry us in your hearts
As we carry you in ours.

❊ ❊ ❊ ❊ ❊

Bless you on your journey
Bless you on your way.
We'll burn a light in the window for you,
And think of you each day.

❊ ❊ ❊ ❊ ❊

The time has come to part
The time has come to leave
The journey's about to start
We are trying not to grieve.

BON VOYAGE! in other words:
German—*gute Reise*
Italian—*buon viaggio* • Spanish—*buen viaje*

Saint Christopher
Patron Saint of Travellers

The legend depicts him as a big strong man devoting his life to carrying travellers across a river. One day a small child asked to be taken on his back across the river to which he agreed, however halfway across the child became so heavy that Christopher was certain they would both drown. The child then revealed that he had been carrying Christ and the sins of the world on his back.

CHRISTENINGS / BAPTISM

Christenings can be religious or non-religious. Some people like to have a baby-naming day to celebrate the newborn's arrival. Whatever is chosen, there is a shared atmosphere of love and well wishing to celebrate the new baby's safe arrival and the promise of its life ahead.

Baptism in the Christian religion is a sacrament that gives over the baby's soul to the Lord. It is a solemn but happy event and is usually followed by a party, which the baby hopefully sleeps through.

Godparents, grandparents or the parents themselves deliver christening toasts. However they can be delivered by anyone present. Etiquette dictates that the very first toast to the christened child be delivered by a godparent, which is followed by a toast from the parents; siblings then receive priority if they wish to give a toast to the new member of their family.

> With parents such as these two
> A child is blessed indeed
> Hugs when he falls
> Kind words to urge him on
> And belief to last him all his days!

❊ ❊ ❊ ❊ ❊

> To the tiniest member of this family
> This party is for you
> Already you've changed our world
> So happy we are about it too.

❊ ❊ ❊ ❊ ❊

A toast to the newest family member
There is nothing like a baby's arrival
To multiply feelings of hope and joy!

❋ ❋ ❋ ❋ ❋

Here's to the happiest days of your life
Spent in the arms of another man's wife—Your mother!

❋ ❋ ❋ ❋ ❋

A toast to the parents of this wee baby
Congratulations and felicitations!
A chance each day to show your love
And bless this treasure from above.

❋ ❋ ❋ ❋ ❋

A blessing on this baby
A blessing on this house.
May there be tears and laughter
And happiness ever after.

❋ ❋ ❋ ❋ ❋

To the newest arrival in the clan
May his feet go pitter-patter
May his voice ring out in joyful tones
May we often hear his laughter.

❋ ❋ ❋ ❋ ❋

To a precious little baby girl
To the gift of her new life
We wish her every happiness
And her parents .. a good night's sleep!

❋ ❋ ❋ ❋ ❋

Lord above, a toast to you
For making me a father!
A son to take care of,
To share in what I know,

To listen and to talk to,
And each day watch him grow.

* * * * *

To my little brother
Who seems so very nice
Hope he doesn't become a bother
Then I'll be thinking twice!

* * * * *

May the angels watch over you
And guide you on your way
May you always be aware,
Of the joy you brought on your birth day.

* * * * *

Here's to the stork a most valuable bird,
Which inhabits the residence districts
He doesn't sing tunes, has no fine plumes
But he certainly helps the statistics!

* * * * *

To my new sister
Welcome to our home
We've waited to meet you, to see you, to greet you
Hope you love me as much as I love you!

* * * * *

To one little baby
We already love,
A gift to us all
From Heaven above.

* * * * *

A toast to the newest member of the family!
A baby will make love stronger, days shorter,
Nights longer, home happier, clothes shabbier,
the past forgotten, and the future worth living for.

✣ ✣ ✣ ✣ ✣

Here's to a baby girl
May she grow to be as lovely
As her mother!

✣ ✣ ✣ ✣ ✣

Here's to the baby
With two tiny hands
That can hold so many hearts.

✣ ✣ ✣ ✣ ✣

Here's to baby! Every day you grow in our hearts,
May you grow to love us as well as we love you.

✣ ✣ ✣ ✣ ✣

Let's drink to the little stranger
Who has entered all our lives
Hard to imagine a time when he/she didn't exist.

✣ ✣ ✣ ✣ ✣

God be in my head,
And in my understanding;
God be in my eyes,
And in my speaking;
God be in my heart,
And in my thinking;
God be at my end,
And at my departing.
—The Sarum Primer

✣ ✣ ✣ ✣ ✣

May joy and peace surround you,
Contentment latch your door,
And happiness be with you now,
And bless you evermore.

* * * * *

Here's to baby! An inestimable blessing and bother!

* * * * *

Lucky stars above you,
Sunshine on your way,
Many friends to love you,
Joy in work and play-
Laughter to outweigh each care,
In your heart a song—
And gladness waiting everywhere
All your whole life long!

* * * * *

God made the world so broad and grand,
Filled with blessings from His hand.
He made the sky so high and blue,
And all the little children too.

* * * * *

Here's to the midwife who delivered you sound
Who handed you first to your mother
God bless her and keep her
Thank God it wasn't left to your father!

* * * * *

Here's a toast to your tiny twins
A double blessing for you,
May your joys be many,
May your struggles be few
May they go to bed when you tell them to!

* * * * *

"The stork has bought a little peach!"
The nurse said with an air,
"I'm mighty glad" the father said,
"He didn't bring a pear."

✵ ✵ ✵ ✵ ✵

A toast to the parents of twins,
Four tiny hands, four tiny feet
Double the treasure, double the treat!

The Sacrament of Baptism
O God, our heavenly Father, grant that this child,
as *he/she* grows in years, may also
grow in grace and in the knowledge of the Lord Jesus Christ,
and that by the restraining and renewing influence
of the Holy Spirit *he/she* may ever be a true child of
thine, serving thee faithfully all of *his/her* days.
So guide and uphold the parents of this child that by
giving care, wise counsel, and holy example, they
may lead *him/her* into that life of faith whose strength
is righteousness and whose fruit is everlasting joy
and peace, through Jesus Christ our Lord.
Amen.

✵ ✵ ✵ ✵ ✵

Godparents
Modern-day godparents are supportive adults whom the parents hope will participate in the child's life.

It is usually seen as a great honour to be chosen as a child's godparent. Some godparents take a special role in the child's life by always remembering birthdays.

The godparent can be family or a close friend and some are equated to legal guardians should the child be orphaned.

CHRISTMAS

Christmas, of all the annual holidays, provides an occasion for merry making, celebrating, gift giving and good wishes to all.

A great toast is in itself a gift! Toasting is the ideal vehicle at Christmas time for showing one's appreciation. There is so much to be thankful for and with family and friends gathered around the table, replete with food and drink, there is a ready audience in the mood for merriment

Why not encourage your children, when they are still young and impressionable, to become accustomed to marking occasions such as these with a few words of their own? There's every chance they'll create a lifelong habit, which will adorn every occasion all the more.

> A toast to you at Christmas time
> A joyful time of year
> It gives us a wonderful excuse
> To gather you all here!
>
> **
>
> Let's toast this time of year
> Joy to the world
> Lots of good cheer
> And family and friends we hold dear.
>
> **
>
> A toast to Santa!
> If you see a fat man ...
> Who's jolly and cute,
> wearing a beard
> and a red flannel suit,

Toast for Life's Occasions

and if he is chuckling
and laughing away,
while flying around
in a miniature sleigh
with eight tiny reindeer
to pull him along,
then lets face it...
Your eggnog's too strong!

❄ ❄ ❄ ❄ ❄

We wish to make a special toast
To _____ our most gracious host
On this Christmas Day
What a wonderful spread and such good cheer
Maybe you'll come to our place next year!

❄ ❄ ❄ ❄ ❄

Here's to you, as good as you are,
Here's to me, as bad as I am,
But as good as you are and as bad as I am,
I'm as good as you are—as bad as I am!
Merry Christmas!

❄ ❄ ❄ ❄ ❄

Christmas is here,
Merry Old Christmas,
Gift-bearing, heart-touching, joy-bringing Christmas,
Day of grand memorie, king of the year.—old Yuletide toast

❄ ❄ ❄ ❄ ❄

A Christmas wish—
May you never forget
what is worth remembering
or remember what is best forgotten.

❄ ❄ ❄ ❄ ❄

May your belly never grumble
May your heart never ache.
May your horse never stumble,
May your cinch never break. —Irish toast

❅ ❅ ❅ ❅ ❅

Yuletide's a time of merriment and mirth
To celebrate the wee babe's birth.

❅ ❅ ❅ ❅ ❅

Here's to our friends, here's to the wine
Here's to the feast upon which we'll dine.

❅ ❅ ❅ ❅ ❅

Let's drink to fine friends,
full hearts and laden table
Let's be of good cheer
As long as we are able!

❅ ❅ ❅ ❅ ❅

Here's to all of us,
Good bless us everyone!
(Tiny Tim's toast from Charles Dickens' A Christmas Carol)

❅ ❅ ❅ ❅ ❅

Now, thrice welcome, Christmas!
Which brings us good cheer,
Mince pies and plum pudding-
Strong ale and strong beer!

❅ ❅ ❅ ❅ ❅

Here's to holly and ivy hanging up,
And to something wet in every cup.

❅ ❅ ❅ ❅ ❅

A Merry Christmas this December
To a lot of folks I don't remember.

❅ ❅ ❅ ❅ ❅

May you never be without a drop at Christmas.
I know I've wished you this before
But every year I wish it more,
A Merry Christmas.

※ ※ ※ ※ ※

Here's wishing you more happiness
Than all my words can tell,
Not just alone for Christmas
But for all the year as well.

※ ※ ※ ※ ※

Let's toast and make merry
It's Christmas time once more
Time for crackers, turkey and stuffing
For good wishes, presents and lights on the tree

※ ※ ※ ※ ※

Let's all raise our glasses
And make a Christmas toast;
To festivities and decorations
Presents being unwrapped first thing in the morning;
To egg nog and punch and crackers with lunch
To full bellies and nodding off.

※ ※ ※ ※ ※

Let's toast the bells on Christmas Day
And those old familiar Christmas carols,
So mild and sweet, the words repeat
Of peace on earth, good will to men.

※ ※ ※ ※ ※

To Father Christmas we make a toast
What a jolly old fellow
Fat round cheeks, flowing beard
And a belly that jiggles like a bowlful of jelly!

※ ※ ※ ※ ※

Class Reunions

School years, the best years of our lives! Hmmm…if that were the case, many of us would not be feeling very optimistic about the years to follow.

Class reunions are interesting gatherings—people have moved on, taken career paths you could not have anticipated. The last time you saw them they were only teenagers filled with hopes and dreams. Now they are mums and dads themselves, responsible citizens, car owners, house owners…or they might have taken a road less travelled!

A toast is a wonderful way to break the ice, to get past that tentative formality and into the affectionate recollections.

> Here's a toast to all who are here
> No matter where you've come from.
> May the best day that you've ever seen
> Be worse than the worst to come!

❊ ❊ ❊ ❊ ❊

> A toast to the kids I knew in school'
> I'd hardly know you now
> You've grown a bit
> Now you're mums and dads
> You've got big jobs
> Can you still remember the fun we had?

❊ ❊ ❊ ❊ ❊

> Here's to our friends we knew in school
> All awkward, timid and spotty
> How far you've come in the passing years
> Good looking, poised and snotty!

❊ ❊ ❊ ❊ ❊

To the Class of...

Here's to our class, here's to our school
Here's to the class of xx—one
Hoping you all achieve in life
Your own brand of success and still have fun.

* * * * *

Here's to our friends, here's to our school,
To the class of xx—two,
Hope your dreams are being fulfiled
And what you say is what you do.

* * * * *

Here's to my school friends,
Here's to the class of xx—three
Wishing you all a fulfilling life
And the best that's yet to be!

* * * * *

Here's to our buddies we knew in school
Here's to the class of xx—four
Good to see you now after all these years
And in the future many more!

* * * * *

Here's to the friends of my school days
To the class of xx—five
How glad am I that we're gathered here
And glad we are still alive!

* * * * *

Here's to my classmates, here's to our school
To the class of xx—six
Here's to all the lessons we learned
The education and the tricks.

* * * * *

Here's to our friends, and to our school
To the class of xx—seven
May your lives be full, may your lives be blessed
And drinks to be served before eleven!

✸ ✸ ✸ ✸ ✸

Here's to the classmates and to the school
To the class of xx—eight
I wish you success in every form
As the dice toss of your fate!

✸ ✸ ✸ ✸ ✸

Here's to the friends from our school
To the class of xx—nine
Here's to old friends and memories
Which improve like vintage wine.

Happy Christmas
In other languages
French—*Joyeux Noel*
German—*Frohe Weihnacht*
Dutch—*Prettige Kernfeest*
Italian—*Buon Natale*
Spanish—*Feliz Navidad*

Easter

Easter is a Christian holiday celebrating Christ's resurrection. It is the holiest of the Christian celebrations. However for some time it has been celebrated in a more secular way and represents spring, renewal and new life. If you don't have some set religious toast or blessing, make your own based on Easter themes.

Some believe the name Easter derives from Oestar, or Eostre, the goddess of spring and renewal. Eggs, as a symbol of renewal, have been around for eons. The Egyptians and Persians dyed eggs and gave them as gifts of renewal.

I am no William Shakespeare
I cannot write a sonnet
But I wish you Happy Easter
And enjoy your Easter bonnet!

✳ ✳ ✳ ✳ ✳ ✳

Let's drink a toast to Easter
To bunnies and egg hunts
Chocolate galore,
Which we all adore
Another holiday just full of fun!

✳ ✳ ✳ ✳ ✳ ✳

Let's toast the hope of Easter
New life and love reborn
The world is saved, our sins repaid
By the sacrifice of One.

✳ ✳ ✳ ✳ ✳ ✳

A happy, joyful Easter
To you and all of yours
Time to bury the hatchet, time to forgive
Not just today but as you live.

✻ ✻ ✻ ✻ ✻

To all our friends at Easter
'tis a lovely time of year
Filled with happiness and hope
And chocolate, never fear!

Happy Easter
How it is said?

Dutch: *Gelukkig Paasfest*
French: *Joyeuses Pâques*
German: *Frohe Ostern*
Italian: *Buona Pasqua*
Portuguese: *Boa Pascoa*
Spanish: *Felices Pascuas*
Swedish: *Glad Påsk*

Eating blessings in different Cultural traditions

Native American
Creator, Earth Mother,
we thank you for our lives and
this beautiful day. Thank You for the bright sun
and the rain we received last night.
Thank You for this circle of friends
and the opportunity to be together.
We want to thank You especially at this time
for the giveaway of their lives made by the
chickens, beets, carrots, grains and lettuce.
We thank them for giving of their lives
so we may continue our lives through this
great blessing. Please help us honour them
through how we live our lives.

* * * * *

Buddhist

(*serving the food*)
In this food I see clearly the presence of the entire universe
supporting my existence. (*looking at the plate of food*)
All living beings are struggling for life.
May they all have enough food to eat today.

(*just before eating*)
The plate is filled with food.
I am aware that each morsel is the fruit of much hard work
by those who produced it.

(beginning to eat)
With the first taste, I promise to practice loving kindness.
With the second, I promise to relieve the suffering of others.
With the third, I promise to see others' joy as my own.
With the fourth, I promise to learn the way of
nonattachment and equanimity.

(after the meal)
The plate is empty.
My hunger is satisfied.
I vow to live for the benefit of all living beings.

✻ ✻ ✻ ✻ ✻

HINDU

Affirmation to my Body
I recognise you are the temple
in which my spirit and creative energy dwell.
I have created you from my need
to have my spirit manifested on earth
so that I may have this time to learn and grow.
I offer you this food so that you may continue
to sustain my creative energy, my spirit, my soul.
I offer this food to you with love,
and a sincere desire for you to remain free
from disease and disharmony.
I accept you as my own creation.
I need you. I love you.

✻ ✻ ✻ ✻ ✻

ISLAMIC

In the name of the compassionate
and beneficent God.

✻ ✻ ✻ ✻ ✻

JUDAIC

Blessed art Thou, O Lord our G-d,
King of the Universe,
Who creates many living
beings and the things they
need. For all that Thou hast
created to sustain
the life of every living
being, blessed be Thou,
the Life of the universe.

* * * * *

CHRISTIAN (GAELIC)

God to enfold me,
God to surround me,
God in my speaking,
God in my thinking,
God in my sleeping,
God in my waking,
God in my watching,
God in my hoping,
God in my life,
God in my lips,
God in my soul,
God in my heart.
God in my sufficing,
God in my slumber,
God in mine ever-lasting soul,
God in mine serenity.

* * * * *

CHRISTIAN GRACE BEFORE MEALS

Come, Lord Jesus, be our Guest,
And let thy gifts to us be blessed.

* * * * *

We thank thee, God, for milk and bread
And all our daily food;
These gifts remind us day by day,
Our Father, thou art good.

* * * * *

Almighty God, you open your hand, and we are fed.
Be at this table, we pray, and bless our family.

* * * * *

God is great, and God is good,
And we thank him for our food;
By his hand we all are fed;
Give us, Lord, our daily bread.

* * * * *

For health and food, for love and friends.
For everything thy goodness sends,
Father, in heaven, we thank thee.

* * * * *

God, we thank you for this food.
For rest and home and all things good.
For wind and rain and sun above.
But most of all for those we love.

* * * * *

Lord, make us truly grateful for the blessings of this day.

* * * * *

Bless these thy gifts, most gracious God,
From whom all goodness springs;
Make clean our hearts and feed our souls
With good and joyful things.

Toast for Life's Occasions

FAMILY REUNIONS

As never before, families have scattered to far-flung parts. Some go to live overseas or interstate because of work, study or an important relationship. Families come in all configurations and have ways of branching out like ivy creeping across every wall face.

> Oh family! There's nothing like it
> The teasing and the goss.
> But if we had to give up any of you
> 'Twould be a terrible loss!

A gathering of clans from time to time, to catch up, meet new partners, see how children have grown, or welcome new arrivals is a great and necessary part of keeping the tapestry of family closely woven.

> To our families
> Who love us despite ourselves
> And are there for us when we are in need!

※ ※ ※ ※ ※

> A toast to my relations
> They are a fantastic bunch
> As lively a crew you never did see
> I'm glad you are all my family!

※ ※ ※ ※ ※

> A toast to the warmth of families
> No matter how big they grow
> From grandparents, aunts and uncles
> To the smallest so-and-so!

※ ※ ※ ※ ※

A toast to family reunions
And sharing in the joy
And seeing all the members
Down to every girl and boy!

❊ ❊ ❊ ❊ ❊

Let's drink to families
No matter how poor a man is
If he has a family he is rich!

❊ ❊ ❊ ❊ ❊

To the family members
We don't get to choose
They are a gift to us
As we are to them!

❊ ❊ ❊ ❊ ❊

A toast to dysfunctional families
Where imperfection reigns
No wonder I feel quite comfortable
And loved for who I am.

❊ ❊ ❊ ❊ ❊

A toast to George Santayana
Who claimed that
A family was nature's masterpiece.

❊ ❊ ❊ ❊ ❊

To the wonderful thing about families
Where you get to meet and know
The people you may never have met
If you hadn't been related!

❊ ❊ ❊ ❊ ❊

A toast to our clan,
a toast to them all
When we are together
We have a ball!

* * * * *

Let's raise our glasses to the family
Link to our past
Bridge to the future!

* * * * *

A toast to George Burns who was very witty:
"Happiness is having a large, loving, caring, close-knit family
… in another city."

* * * * *

A toast to the thing called family
May we ever be part of one,
And welcome all newcomers
In-laws, outlaws and the tiniest one!

* * * * *

A toast to our family
Fathers, mothers, sisters and brothers
Nephews and nieces, uncles and aunts
Big ones, small ones, old ones, poor ones
God bless us all!

* * * * *

FATHERS DAY

Father's Day is an opportunity to deliver a heartfelt toast to a very special person who has taken on what is conceivably one of the hardest roles to play in life. Say what's in your heart.

Here's to my dad
If I can become half the man that he is
I will have achieved greatness.

* * * * *

Let's toast my father
Who's been there for me every day of my life
I am so grateful to you!

* * * * *

To my dad,
You picked me up when I fell down
And taught me how to ride my bike
You helped me learn to drive the car
Then bought me one of my own.
Thank you for everything!

* * * * *

Here's to our father
The best man we know!
He's taken care of all of us
And never counted the cost.
We hope that when we're parents
We can be even half as good as you!

* * * * *

To our darling dad
A man whom we all love
Who always listened to our calls for help
And was there to sort things out.
Who loved us steadily every day
Taught us what the world was about.

* * * * *

Happy Father's Day
We're glad we are related
To such a wonderful man
Your wisdom has brushed off on us
As has your example.
One day if we follow you
We'll be great parents to our kids too.

* * * * *

Dad, it wasn't until I had kids of my own
I started to realise
That being a father is really quite tough.
It takes patience and love and good sense.
I'm blessed that I have your example to follow
And able to ask your advice.
Thank you for everything!

* * * * *

FELLOW WORKERS

Whether we like it or not, work is one of life's realities. One could safely say that most of us work to live and not the other way around. However it's the colleagues and friends we make at work that make our work day bearable and sometimes quite enjoyable. So here's to toasting those fine people.

> To my fellow workers
> We've made some profit
> We've made some loss
> We've made them both
> Despite our boss.

✽ ✽ ✽ ✽ ✽

> Too much work, and no vacation,
> Deserves at least a small libation.
> So hail my friends and raise your glasses;
> Work is the curse of the drinking classes.

✽ ✽ ✽ ✽ ✽

> To my fellow workers
> We work in the trenches
> Day after day.
> Your friendship makes it all worthwhile
> It's certainly not the pay.

✽ ✽ ✽ ✽ ✽

> To my colleagues
> Who share this working life
> All its highs, all the strife!
> May we always be able to see
> The humour no matter the tragedy!

✽ ✽ ✽ ✽ ✽

FRIENDSHIP

How could one not have special toasts for friends? After all, nearly all life's good times will be celebrated with our friends. Never to be taken for granted, those people who take pleasure in your company and are there for you when you need them, why not make a friendly toast to your friends when you get together?

My heart is as full as my glass,
When I drink to you, old friend!

✻ ✻ ✻ ✻ ✻

Here's to a good friend:
They know you well and like you just the same.

✻ ✻ ✻ ✻ ✻

My dearest friend
This toast's for you,
Who's always on my side
And yet will tell me when I'm wrong
Despite the rocky ride!

✻ ✻ ✻ ✻ ✻

Here's to our friends, and the strength to put up with them.

✻ ✻ ✻ ✻ ✻

To my good friends
Who know me but love me anyway!

✻ ✻ ✻ ✻ ✻

To my very good friend
Who walked in when the rest of the world walked out.

✻ ✻ ✻ ✻ ✻

Here's to good friends
May our misunderstandings be written in sand
Our fellow-feeling in marble.

* * * * *

My friends are the best friends loyal, willing and able.
Now let's get to drinking, glasses off the table!

* * * * *

Here's to a sweetheart, a bottle and a friend.
The first is beautiful, the second full,
and the last ever faithful.

* * * * *

Good friends to sit at my table
Good friends to share the wine,
The laughter the tears
All through our years,
People who make living worthwhile!

* * * * *

To my dearest friend
Who's had a tough year
Here's hoping the dark clouds will lift
And the sunshine will appear.

* * * * *

To friendship
Which is not blind,
But merely chooses to close its eyes.

* * * * *

Friends we are today,
And friends we'll always be —
For I am wise to you,
And you can see through me.

* * * * *

May your home always be too small to hold all your friends.

※ ※ ※ ※ ※

To my dearest friend
Who has the courage
To tell me my faults
In private.

※ ※ ※ ※ ※

To friendship!
There are only two things worthwhile in life
Shared laughter and the love of good friends.

※ ※ ※ ※ ※

To the ship that never founders
To the ship that carries you through storms
To friendship!

※ ※ ※ ※ ※

To friendship
The gift we give ourselves!

※ ※ ※ ※ ※

A toast to friends who are faithful
A toast to ye who are kind,
I know you'd come running
Just as I would for you,
There's nothing, just nothing we wouldn't do.

※ ※ ※ ※ ※

To toast to old friends
Let's drink to the new
Don't know what my life would be like
If I didn't know you!

※ ※ ※ ※ ※

To the people we love to spend time with,
The ones we call our friends

Drink up, laugh long,
And if you feel one coming on,
Give us all a song!

* * * * *

I drink to your charm,
your beauty and your brains—
Which gives you a rough idea of how hard up I am
for a drink. — Groucho Marx

* * * * *

Mark Twain said it well
"To get the full value of joy
You must have someone to divide it with."

* * * * *

Here's to you, my honest friend,
Wishing these hard times would mend.

* * * * *

Friendship's the wine of life.
Let's drink of it and to it.

* * * * *

May friendship, like wine, improve as time advances,
And may we always have old wine, old friends, and young cares.

* * * * *

Here's to you and here's to me,
Friends may we always be!
But, if by chance we disagree,
Up yours! Here's to me!

* * * * *

May the friends of our youth be the companions of our old age.

* * * * *

May you live as long as you like,
And have all you like as long as you live.

✣ ✣ ✣ ✣ ✣

There are good ships,
and there are wood ships,
The ships that sail the sea.
But the best ships, are friendships,
And may they always be.

✣ ✣ ✣ ✣ ✣

May the saddest day of your future be no worse
than the happiest day of your past.

✣ ✣ ✣ ✣ ✣

May all your troubles be little ones.

✣ ✣ ✣ ✣ ✣

May neighbours respect you,
Trouble neglect you,
The angels protect you,
And heaven accept you.

✣ ✣ ✣ ✣ ✣

May you have the hindsight to know where you've been,
The foresight to know where you are going,
And the insight to know when you have gone too far.

✣ ✣ ✣ ✣ ✣

May you be poor in misfortune, rich in blessings,
Slow to make enemies and quick to make friends.
And may you know nothing but happiness from this day forward.

✣ ✣ ✣ ✣ ✣

May you have warm words on a cold evening,
a full moon on a dark night,
and a smooth road all the way to your door.

✣ ✣ ✣ ✣ ✣

May the rooms of our friendship never go musty
May the hinges of our friendship never grow rusty.

※ ※ ※ ※ ※

Here's to you and yours,
And to mine and ours,
And if mine and ours ever come
Across you and yours,
I hope you and yours will do
As much for mine and ours,
As mine and ours have done
For you and yours!

※ ※ ※ ※ ※

May the hand of a friend always be near you, and may God fill your heart with gladness to cheer you.

※ ※ ※ ※ ※

May fortune still be kind to you, and happiness be true to you, and life be long and good to you, is the toast of all our friends to you.

※ ※ ※ ※ ※

We get by with a little help from our friends
Here's hoping their caring never ends!

※ ※ ※ ※ ※

Graduation

Graduation is a major educational accomplishment in a person's life and is often marked with a party to celebrate the occasion. It's a great opportunity to give thanks, to acknowledge the graduate and what it has taken to get them to this point. Why not propose a toast...to the graduate, to the parents, the teachers, to learning itself?

High school graduation

Your school years are over
Congratulations and well done!
Your family knows how hard you've worked
The teachers feel their work is done.

* * * * *

School days, misrule days
The books and the classes
We toast to their passing
And a bright future for the scholar.

* * * * *

A toast to the teachers
Who taught every day
A toast to their patience
Their learning and care.
If not for these people
You'd never be here!

* * * * *

It is often said that parents
Go through all the steps
As if they were graduating all over again
When one of theirs is finishing school.
A toast to mum and dad!

* * * * *

UNIVERSITY GRADUATION

To our new graduate
You might think your degree is a ticket to the good life
But why don't you think of it primarily
As a ticket to change the world.

* * * * *

Let's drink to the Earl of Chesterfield who wrote:
"Wear your learning like your watch
In a private pocket
And do not pull it out and strike it
Merely to show
That you have one."

* * * * *

Benjamin Disraeli once said: "A university should be a place of light, liberation and learning. Here's to your enlightenment, your liberation and your knowledge!"

* * * * *

Epictetus was a stoical Greek who said: " We are not to give credit to the many who say that none ought to be educated but the free; look instead to the philosophers who say that the well-educated alone are free."

* * * * *

To our new graduate!
For as long as you've lived we've believed in you, Despite the times when you really didn't know what to do. And now you're a graduate, not a bit scrappy, You'll get a fine job and make us all happy!

✫ ✫ ✫ ✫ ✫

Let's toast Albert Einstein who said
"The important thing is never to stop questioning."

✫ ✫ ✫ ✫ ✫

To the new graduate:
If opportunity doesn't knock, just build a door.

✫ ✫ ✫ ✫ ✫

To Lord Brougham who claimed:
"Education makes people easy to lead, but difficult to drive Easy to govern but impossible to enslave."

✫ ✫ ✫ ✫ ✫

This day is the biggest day of your life,
It's yours and yours alone.
Now go out and find a job my friend
And pay off your student loan.

✫ ✫ ✫ ✫ ✫

To the graduate,
You have done the hard yards and you've finished the course.
Congratulations on this wonderful accomplishment and all the best
For a wonderful future.

✫ ✫ ✫ ✫ ✫

GUESTS

What would any celebration be without guests? They are the witnesses to life's occasions and milestones, friends and well-wishers, God bless them every one. It is quite fitting to show appreciation for the people who willingly gather to share in life's milestones and celebrations.

>Here's to our guest –
>Don't let him rest
>But keep the elbow bending.
>The time to drink
>Full time to think
>Tomorrow—when you're mending!

* * * * *

>You are welcome here
>Be at your ease,
>Get up when you're ready
>Go to bed when you please.

* * * * *

>To our guests,
>The ornament of a house is the guests who frequent it.

* * * * *

>To our guests,
>You don't have to thank us
>Or laugh at our jokes
>Sit deep and come often
>You're one of the folks.

* * * * *

>A toast to our guests all gathered here
>You are very welcome any time of year!

* * * * *

Toast for Life's Occasions

Happy to share with you
Such as we've got
The mouldy old bread
Porridge in the pot.

✻ ✻ ✻ ✻ ✻

A toast to our honoured guest
With whose presence we've been blessed!
Raise your glasses and have good cheer,
We are so lucky to have you here!

✻ ✻ ✻ ✻ ✻

May all who sit at this our table
Drink and eat as long as you're able!
And when you have run out of puff
You're getting weary, you've had enough
We'll ply you with coffee and send you…off!

✻ ✻ ✻ ✻ ✻

Let's raise our glass and toast ye all
We hope you've really had a ball!
It's been such fun to have you here,
To share the feast, to drink the beer.

✻ ✻ ✻ ✻ ✻

A toast to all who share our table,
Our friends and family, we're glad you were able
To come this evening, no special date,
Just being together…cause to celebrate!

✻ ✻ ✻ ✻ ✻

May all who came to share this meal,
Break bread with us, it's no big deal
We wish you all in life that's best,
And thank you for just being our guest!

✻ ✻ ✻ ✻ ✻

HEN'S NIGHT

Girls have their own brand of fun, and it generally tends to be more subdued than when the boys get together. This doesn't rule out collective devil-may—careness. The girls may decide to let their hair down with wine, wit and waywardness, and in that situation there's no telling what kinds of toasts they might make. The following are quite tame compared.

A toast to the blushing bride
This time next week she'll be going for a ride.

* * * * *

May you always be happy
And live at your ease
Get a kind husband
And do as you please!

* * * * *

A toast to the bride-soon-to-be
Two things to remember you'll see
When you're wrong, admit it
And when you're right, shut up!

* * * * *

To Mr Right
Just make sure his first name isn't Always!

* * * * *

Here's to _____ (bride's name)
Who knows all her new husband's favourite foods ...
And where to order them!

* * * * *

Here's to the men we love
And here's to the men who love us
And if the men we love don't love us
Then forget the men. Here's to us!

* * * * *

To the secret of a happy marriage
Let him deal with the big decisions
So you can deal with the small ones,
And make sure they're all small!

* * * * *

A toast to the girl who's getting hitched
We're here to say goodbye
To your empty days and the single life
This time next week you'll be a wife!

* * * * *

A toast to our single friend
Who's soon to be a bride!
Just remember this, through thick and thin
We'll always take your side!

* * * * *

A toast to our dear bride-to-be
No need for pre-wedding jitters
There's nothing at all to worry about
We've all agreed to be babysitters!

* * * * *

A toast to our friend who's getting wed,
To becoming a fine man's Missus
To a cosy home and a nice soft bed
To loving words and passionate kisses!

* * * * *

HISTORICAL TOASTS

Here is a collection of toasts gathered from history's pages. Comforting to discover that despite the world changing so radically we still love to gather in groups, share conversation, food and wine and…we still love to toast the occasion!

Toast of 1675
Love and wine are the bonds that fasten us all,
The world but for these to confusion would fall,
Were it not for the pleasures of love and good wine,
Mankind, for each trifle their lives would resign;
They'd not value dull life nor could live without thinking,
Nor would kings rule the world but for love and good drinking.

* * * * *

Jacobite toast
God bless the king, I mean the Faith's defender,
God bless _____ no harm to blessing—the Pretender,
But which is Pretender, and which is King?
God bless us all, that's quite another thing.

* * * * *

Sailor's toast, 1795
When lifting high the rosy glass,
Each comrade toasts his favourite lass
And to his fond bosom near;
Ah, how can I the nectar sip,
Or Anna's name escape my lip
When Mary is my dear?

* * * * *

**Horatio Nelson's Navy, in the officer's wardroom
The first toast was always to the King, and after that to each day of the week in this order:**

Monday: "Our ships at sea."
Tuesday: "Our men."
Wednesday: "Ourselves."
Thursday: "A bloody war or a sickly season."
Friday: "A willing foe and sea room."
Saturdays: "Sweethearts and wives."
Sundays: "Absent friends."

✻ ✻ ✻ ✻ ✻

**Andrew Jackson's motto,
a toast often used in the nineteenth century:**

Ask nothing that is not clearly right, and submit to nothing that is wrong.

✻ ✻ ✻ ✻ ✻

Nineteenth century toast often directed to Queen Victoria, which over time became shortened to "Cheers!":

Nine times, nine cheers!

✻ ✻ ✻ ✻ ✻

Irish toast, early twentieth century:

Ireland—St Patrick destroyed its creeping things of other days—may his disciples speedily exterminate the political reptiles of the present age.

✻ ✻ ✻ ✻ ✻

French cavalry toast, World War I:

To our women, our horses and the men who ride them.

✻ ✻ ✻ ✻ ✻

HOSTS AND HOSTESSES

An essential feature of most social events is the host/hostess. If not for their good graces, the celebration would not be possible. Remembering the etiquette of toasting, it falls to the host to give the first toast of the gathering, then it is only fair to reply by delivering a toast to the host. Here are some suggestions.

> A toast for our gracious host
> We all agree,
> ' twas a great part-ee
> And may he come, be it night or morn
> And be a guest to all of us!

> * * * * *

> To our host,
> An excellent man;
> For is not a man
> Fairly judged by the
> Company he keeps?

> * * * * *

> What's a table richly spread
> Without a woman at its head?

> * * * * *

> To our hostess, what a gem!
> May her home be blessed, her children able,
> And many gather round her table!

> * * * * *

Here's a toast to you and yours
Not forgetting me and mine.
The food was delicious and so was the wine!

* * * * *

A toast to our hostess
So patient and sweet.
But now that we're gathered
When can we eat?

* * * * *

To our gracious hostess
May your house be bright and gay
May your children clean away
And your husband bless the day
That you invited your friends!

* * * * *

To the grapes that grew
To their juice that turned to wine,
To the host who popped the cork
And made it yours and mine!

* * * * *

Let's drink to the maker of this feast
To the food and wine and cheer.
May his generosity see
Many happy returns!

* * * * *

To your welcome which was quite cordial
To your cordial, which is very welcome!

* * * * *

We drink to your home
We drink to your table
We drink to your cellar
As long as we're able!

✻ ✻ ✻ ✻ ✻

We raise our glasses and thank you both
For opening your home and sharing your fare,
You really are a generous pair!

✻ ✻ ✻ ✻ ✻

Let's drink to the feast maker
May his generosity be rewarded!

✻ ✻ ✻ ✻ ✻

To the man who sits at the top of the table
We drink to you whilst we are able!
Long may you want to invite us here
To eat and drink and be of good cheer!

✻ ✻ ✻ ✻ ✻

Let's raise a glass be it beer or wine
And drink a toast to thee and thine!
Your children are sweet, and so's your wife
We love being invited to be part of your life!

✻ ✻ ✻ ✻ ✻

House warming

Moving house is a modern day reality. For some it happens very often. To gather one's friends as a blessing on the new abode is a great way to celebrate the making of a house into a home.

Make the occasion special by delivering a toast, as the host or as a guest.

A toast to our friends in our new home
May you always know you can beat a path to our door.

* * * * *

To those we love
Mi casa, su casa—which means
Our home is your home.

* * * * *

To your new home—
The father's castle
The child's haven
The mother's world.

* * * * *

A toast to our gracious hosts
May these walls ring with chatter and laughter
May the halls fill with good friends and true.

* * * * *

A blessing on your new house
Even though the walls are bare
With light at the windows
It has a welcoming air.
Never mind before you know it,

Your house will be a home
With food upon the table
Flowers and a lawn
A fire and an easy chair
And friends to depend upon.

* * * * *

May our home always be too small
To hold all our friends.

* * * * *

To your new home
May the roof above you never fall in
And the good people beneath it never fall out!

* * * * *

A toast to beginning!
It takes a whole lot of living in a house to make it a home,
let's get it off to a good start.

* * * * *

A toast to our good friends
Assembled here tonight;
Thank you for helping to celebrate
The beginning of life in our new home.

* * * * *

We toast the new homeowners,
May there be laughter and warmth and nice things to say,
Enough to eat, drink and less work, more play
Friends to share, and help in any way.
Look back in years and bless this day.

* * * * *

A blessing on your home
Walls to keep out the wind,
And a roof to keep out the rain,

And drinks beside the fire -
Laughter to cheer you
And those you love near you,
And all that your heart may desire!

* * * * *

A toast to the pleasures of home:
A good book, a bright light and an easy chair.

* * * * *

May blessings be upon your house
Your roof, and hearth and walls
May there be lights to welcome you
When evening's shadow falls
The love that like the guiding star
Still signals when you roam
A book, a friend—these are the things
That make a house a home.—Irish toast

* * * * *

A toast to the making of a home
Where everyone inside the walls
Feels at ease upon the couch,
No need to stand on ceremony
Act like themselves, not afraid to slouch.

* * * * *

Home is where you hang your hat
Home is where you'd find a cat
Home is where your family are
Home is where you park your car.
But the thing that makes a house a home
Is the love that's waiting whenever you roam.

* * * * *

MOTHERS DAY

It is said that the bond between mother and child is the most important and abiding in any person's life. How fitting then to toast the mother on her special day.

A toast to our mum
Hip! Hip! Hooray!
Much love from your kids on Mother's Day!

※ ※ ※ ※ ※

Let's raise our glasses and make a toast
To the mum whom we all love the most!

※ ※ ※ ※ ※

To our mum
Who keeps loving us
Even when we deserve it the least!

※ ※ ※ ※ ※

We have toasted our futures
Our friends and our wives,
We have toasted each other
Wishing all happy lives.
But I tell you my friends
This toast beats all others
So raise your glasses once more
In a toast for—our mothers!

※ ※ ※ ※ ※

To the most precious gift of all
And one we can scarcely live without
A mother's love!

※ ※ ※ ※ ※

Let's toast our mother.
She gave us life
Then loved us every single day.
She kept us warm and fed
She gave us advice
Which we didn't always heed,
But here she remains our friend in need.

※ ※ ※ ※ ※

A toast to my dearest mum
Who kept believing in me
Through obstacles and setbacks.
That confidence sustained me.
Thank you, mum!

※ ※ ※ ※ ※

To my mum,
Who always believed in me

※ ※ ※ ※ ※

A toast to motherhood
All love begins and ends there.

※ ※ ※ ※ ※

To my dearest mum,
No matter how middle-aged her children get
She is always watching out for signs of improvement.

※ ※ ※ ※ ※

To being a mum,
There is nothing easier or harder
Nothing more rewarding or frustrating
More capable of giving joy or pain,
Who would miss it for the world?

※ ※ ※ ※ ※

A toast to my mum
It wasn't till I became one myself
That I realised how patient, thoughtful
Generous, understanding you need to be,
On any given day, and even then
Your kids might still blame it on you!

※ ※ ※ ※ ※

To my mum,
Other women may come and go
But my love for you goes on forever!

※ ※ ※ ※ ※

To the woman who held me close to her heart
Even before my real birthday
Who's been there for me through bad and good
Who's loved me better than a mother could!

※ ※ ※ ※ ※

To motherhood,
May we always honour the woman who
Loves us better than all others do!

※ ※ ※ ※ ※

May your children love you,
As you deserve!
Wholly and deeply,
Without reserve!

※ ※ ※ ※ ※

"Naughty but nice" toasts

Occasionally, depending on the friends you have gathered together and the tone of the evening and maybe the amount of alcoholic beverage collectively consumed, it is quite apt for the toasts to take a slightly wicked turn. Here is a sampling:

Bottoms up!	Here's to it.	Here's 2 U,
Tops down	If you get to it	Here's 2 Me,
Wear a smile	And can't do it,	Here's 2 Sex,
Not a frown.	Call on me,	When It's Free!
	I'm used to it.	

* * * * *

Here's to the girl with the big blue eyes,
Here's to the girl with the milk-white thighs
Our eyes have met; our thighs not yet.
Here's hoping!

* * * * *

Be good.
If you can't be good, be careful;
And if you can't be careful,
Name it after me.

* * * * *

Here's to birthdays.
Birthday's only come once a year.
Aren't you glad you're not a birthday?

* * * * *

Man on top of woman hasn't long to stay.
His head is full of business and his ass is full of play.
He goes in like a lion and comes out like a lamb.
He buttons up his pants and doesn't give a damn.

* * * * *

May you always come more than you go.

✫ ✫ ✫ ✫ ✫

Here's to that which goes in hard & stiff
and comes out soft & wet.
Here's to...bubblegum.

✫ ✫ ✫ ✫ ✫

Here's to the universe of man,
They've done it since the world began.
Robins and wrens do it,
Chickens and hens do it,
Kings and queens do it,
And I'd do it too if
I hadn't promised not to.
For I'd get fat if
I ate cake like you do.

✫ ✫ ✫ ✫ ✫

Dogs do it, cats do it,
monkeys have a try.
Mums do it, dads do it,
so why don't you and I?

✫ ✫ ✫ ✫ ✫

Here's to men:
When I meet them, I like them.
When I like them, I kiss them.
When I kiss them, I love them.
When I love them, I let them.
When I let them, I lose them.
God damn them!

✫ ✫ ✫ ✫ ✫

Here's to the night I met you.
If I hadn't met you, I wouldn't have let you.

Now that I let you, I'm glad that I met you.
And I'll let you again, I bet you!

*****

A man may kiss his wife goodbye,
The rose may kiss the butterfly,
The wine may kiss the frosted glass,
And you, my friends, may kiss my ass.

*****

Here's to the game called 'Ten Toes'
That's played all over town.
The women play with ten toes up.
And the men with ten toes down!

*****

Here's to me in my sober mood,
When I ramble, sit, and think.
Here's to me in my drunken mood,
When I gamble, sin, and drink.
And when my days are over,
And from this world I pass,
I hope they bury me upside down,
So the world can kiss my…arse!

*****

Here's to an hour of sweet repose,
Tummy to tummy and toes to toes,
Then after an hour of such delight,
It's fanny to fanny for the rest of the night.

*****

Here's to the camel
Who's sexual desire is greater than anyone thinks.
One night in a moment of sexual madness
It tried to make love to the Sphinx.

But the Sphinx's posterior opening
Was clogged with the sands of the Nile,
Which accounts for the hump on the camel
And the Sphinx's inscrutable smile.

* * * * *

Here's to the Hereafter.
If you're not here after
What I'm here after,
You'll be here a long time after I'm gone.

* * * * *

Here's to the top
And here's to the middle
Let's hope tonight
We all get a little.

* * * * *

Here's to the policeman who passes our way.
Here's to the mailman who calls every day.
Here's to the babies who continually say:
"Mom, which is my daddy—the blue or the grey?"

* * * * *

Here's to you, and here's to me,
Here's to the girl with the dimpled knee.
Here's to the boy who fastened her garter;
It wasn't much—but a damned good starter!

* * * * *

Here's to the bee that stung the bull
That started the bull to bucking
Here's to Adam who ate the first apple
And started the world to...Eating apples!

* * * * *

Here's to the Scots, Irish and Picts,
"Don't piss us off or we'll cut of your...Wassail!"

* * * * *

Here's to when I want it,
And I want it bad,
And if I don't get it
It makes me mad,
And if I do get it
It makes me frisky,
Now don't get me wrong
'Cause I mean whiskey.

* * * * *

The boy stood on the burning deck,
The deck was made of brass (glass)
The boy slipped on the burning deck
And landed on his—
Don't be mistaken, don't be misled,
The boy slipped on the burning deck
And landed on his head.

* * * * *

May you live as long as you want to;
May you want to as long as you live.
If I'm asleep when you want to, wake me;
If I'm awake and don't want to, make me.

* * * * *

Here's to me and here's to you,
And if in the world
There was just us two
And I could promise that nobody knew
Would you?

* * * * *

Let's drink to kissing—
Kiss beneath the garden gate,
Kiss beneath the rose.
The proper place to kiss a girl,
Is between the head and toes.

* * * * *

Here's to the bride
who's still a virgin.
Her hormones
are really surgin'.

* * * * *

Here's to the groom,
who'll skip the dinner.
'Stead he'll stick'
his winner in 'er.

* * * * *

NEW YEARS

New Years Eve is a holiday to celebrate renewal and the beginning of a brand new year. It's a time for optimism, hope and resolutions. We find ourselves promising to change behaviours that need changing, and to start things off we attend a big party—the 'eat, drink and make merry' kind! In fact if we hadn't partied so hard we might have had less to repent! Make a toast to the promise and the promises in the spirit of the festivity!

> Let's drink to human failings
> Our stuff-ups and mistakes,
> And remember to err is human
> But to forgive oneself feels divine!

> A toast we make
> to New Year's resolutions
> When all is said and done
> Much more is said than done!

> Happy New Year!
> Be of good cheer!
> Drink up the wine, if not the beer.

> To our friends all gathered here
> To celebrate a bright New Year
> May there be good fortune, love and laughter
> And no hangover the morning after!

A toast to our resolutions, big and small,
And if by some mistake
Our promises we break
Let's brush ourselves off and move on.

※ ※ ※ ※ ※

Let's toast to the year that is gone
With a new one coming on
Grateful we are
To have come this far!

※ ※ ※ ※ ※

To New Year's Resolutions
Whichever ones you make
Being kinder, lighter, brighter
Funnier, friendlier, busier
Wealthier…or taking a break.
Good luck!

※ ※ ※ ※ ※

To absent friends we oft' should drink
And hope they're doing fine.
Of those who've passed we oft should think
For the sake of Auld Lang Syne.

※ ※ ※ ※ ※

A Happy New Year to all assembled here
As we count down to a new beginning
Enjoy this night of celebration
And a future where you're winning.

※ ※ ※ ※ ※

Let's all drink up as we need the courage
To keep our resolutions.

※ ※ ※ ※ ※

Let's drink to Aldous Huxley who said:
"There's only one corner of the Universe
You can be certain of improving
And that's … yourself!"

✧ ✧ ✧ ✧ ✧

To ghost of year past
And spectre of year to come.

✧ ✧ ✧ ✧ ✧

And so we drink to Father Time
Curer of our sorrows,
Who has wings, and waits for no man
Dear Time, please grant us more tomorrows.

✧ ✧ ✧ ✧ ✧

Let's drink to the present moment
What's past is gone
And the future is still to come
Let's celebrate NOW!

✧ ✧ ✧ ✧ ✧

Here's to making a resolution
To be at least as kind to yourself
As you would be to your best friend!

✧ ✧ ✧ ✧ ✧

To promises made and promises kept
May we drink to following through.

✧ ✧ ✧ ✧ ✧

Let's raise our glasses
To a New Year full of hope.

✧ ✧ ✧ ✧ ✧

Here's a toast to the future,
A toast to the past,
And a toast to our friends, far and near.

May the future be pleasant;
The past a bright dream;
May our friends remain faithful and dear.

※ ※ ※ ※ ※

As we start the New Year,
Let's get down on our knees
to thank God we're on our feet.

※ ※ ※ ※ ※

Here's to a bright New Year
And a fond farewell to the old;
Here's to things that are yet to come
And to the memories that we hold.

※ ※ ※ ※ ※

In the New Year,
May your right hand always
be stretched out in friendship,
but never in want.

※ ※ ※ ※ ※

The New Year is ringing in,
May he be bringing in
The Good Times we've waited for so long in vain!
Without the demanding,
All rise and drink standing,
And so say we all of us again and again.

※ ※ ※ ※ ※

Let us be merry, merry here,
While we're all merry, merry here;
For who can know where we shall go
To be merry another year.

※ ※ ※ ※ ※

A song for the old, while its knell is tolled,
And its parting moments fly!
But a song and a cheer for the glad New Year,
While we watch the old year die!

* * * * *

Welcome be ye that are here,
Welcome all, and make good cheer,
Welcome all, another year.

* * * * *

Ring out the old, ring in the new,
Ring, happy bells, across the snow:
The year is going, let him go;
Ring out the false, ring in the true.

* * * * *

Here's to the year that has gone
With its share of joy and sadness
And here's to the year to come
May it have a full measure of gladness.

* * * * *

Stir the eggnog, lift the toddy,
Happy New Year, everybody. — Phyllis McGinley

* * * * *

Cheers to you, Cheers to me,
Have a Happy New Year's Eve!

* * * * *

For last year's words belong to last year's language
And next year's words await another voice.
And to make an end is to make a beginning. — T.S. Eliot

* * * * *

Each age has deemed the new-born year
The fittest time for festal cheer. — Sir Walter Scott

※ ※ ※ ※ ※

Youth is when you're allowed to stay up late on New Year's
Eve. Middle age is when you're forced to. — Bill Vaughn

※ ※ ※ ※ ※

Ring out the old, ring in the new,
Ring, happy bells, across the snow:
The year is going, let him go;
Ring out the false, ring in the true. — Lord Alfred Tennyson

※ ※ ※ ※ ※

Always bear in mind that your own resolution to succeed is
more important than any one thing. — Abraham Lincoln

※ ※ ※ ※ ※

The future belongs to those who believe
in the beauty of their dreams. — Eleanor Roosevelt

Happy New Year
In other languages

Dutch: *Gelukkig Nieujaar*
French: *Bonne Annee*
German: *Ein gutes neues Jaar*
Italian: *Buon Anno*
Spanish: *Feliz Ano Nuevo*

Top 10 New Years Resolutions

1. MORE time with family and friends
2. MORE fitness
3. LESS bulge
4. QUIT smoking
5. ENJOY life more
6. QUIT drinking
7. LESS debt
8. LEARN something new
9. HELP others
10. GET organised

OCCUPATION

Caught for subjects upon which to toast your friends and colleagues? Here are a few suggestions based on their occupation:

Actors
To actors,
Who spend all their time trying to do
What they put you in asylums for.

Advertising
To the ad man,
There is no such thing as bad publicity
except your own obituary.

Architect
Here's to the architect. Frank Lloyd once said:
"The physician can bury his mistakes, but the architect can only advise the client to plant vines".

Artist
A toast to the artist:
whose gift is never seeing things as they really are.

Banker
A toast to the banker, in the words of Mark Twain:
"The banker is the fellow who lends his umbrella when the sun is shining but wants it back the moment it rains."

Barber
Our hair he cuts
And shaves our face
And talks and talks
With ease and grace!

* * * * *

Computer person
A toast to our computer whiz
To err is human, but to really stuff things up
Requires a computer.

* * * * *

Cook
A toast to a wonderful cook,
Who is able to make a feast out of whatever there is in the fridge
Able to throw a pinch of this and a peck of that in
To make the meal delicious.

* * * * *

Dentist
A drink to the dentist we make
Who, East, West, North or South
Always lives from hand to mouth.

* * * * *

Doctor
Unto our doctors let us drink
Who cure our ills and chills.
No matter what we really think
Of their pills and bills!

* * * * *

Firefighter
May he never be toasted except by the glass of his friends!

* * * * *

Gardener
May the weeds all wilt before you
May the veggies thrive and prosper
And may the bugs choose another patch
So you can rest instead!

※ ※ ※ ※ ※

Lawyer
Here's to the man/ woman of great trials and many convictions.

※ ※ ※ ※ ※

Media
A health to the slaves of the masses
Who careless of fortune or fame;
Will give their best years, missing brilliant careers
And all for the love of the game!

※ ※ ※ ※ ※

Military
A toast to the soldier amongst us
Don't ever be the first, don't ever be the last
And don't ever volunteer for anything!

※ ※ ※ ※ ※

Musician
To music,
The only sensual pleasure without vice.

※ ※ ※ ※ ※

Police
Let's toast the policeman and making ends meet:
"Yeah, we have a quota. Two more tickets and my wife gets a toaster oven".

※ ※ ※ ※ ※

Politician
A toast to our politician,

To the gift of speaking with conviction
without saying anything at all.

✻ ✻ ✻ ✻ ✻

Psychiatrist
Here's to the shrink,
He finds you cracked and leaves you stony broke!

✻ ✻ ✻ ✻ ✻

Sales
Let's drink to our profit and loss,
Which'll give us an excuse to put the drink
on the expense account!

✻ ✻ ✻ ✻ ✻

Teacher
A toast to the best kind of teacher we know,
A mediocre teacher tells. A good teacher explains.
A great teacher demonstrates. This excellent teacher inspires.

✻ ✻ ✻ ✻ ✻

Waiter
We drink your health, O Waiter
And may you persevere
Through gout, old age or sudden death
Well, at least till supper's served!

✻ ✻ ✻ ✻ ✻

Writing
To the writer
'tis the hardest way to earn a living
With the exception of wrestling alligators!

✻ ✻ ✻ ✻ ✻

Recovering from Illness

When someone is recovering from an illness, it may not be a good idea to mix alcohol with any medication they may be on. Fill the patient's glass with juice, broth or cold water, but there's no reason why you can't have a tipple!

Illness can come at any time, always uninvited,
So good to see you on the road to recovery!

* * * * *

Here's to saying goodbye to ill health
To hospital food, nurses and tubes.
In no time at all you'll be your old self.

* * * * *

To our dearest friend who's on the mend
We're so happy to see you coming good!

* * * * *

A toast to you and your getting well,
We're here to speed the process
With TLC and laughter
And lots of looking after.

* * * * *

A toast to our patient patient
Who's put up with feeling crook,
Now the fever has broken, you're smiling again
We're so happy you've turned the bend!

* * * * *

Here's to laughter
They say it's the best medicine
So we're here to tickle your fancy!

* * * * *

Retirement

Sooner or later if you're lucky, the time comes to retire from working for a living. Whether you can afford it or not, is another matter.

The retirement party is a great opportunity for the retiree to say precisely what they please, finally, about their erstwhile employer. Not that many do, it's simply knowing that you could if you felt inclined!

>Throw out the alarm clock,
>The suit and the shiny shoes,
>Put up your feet
>No more work blues!

>Four blessings upon you...
>Older whiskey
>Younger women [men]
>Faster horses
>More money.

>It's with joy and sadness
>that we say farewell tonight
>No one more loved or respected
>has earned this right.

>May all your joys be pure joys,
>and all your pain champagne.

You now have the freedom to do all the things you spent the last forty years dreaming of doing.

Here's to the holidays—all 365 of them!

When you're sitting at home with nothing to do. Think of all of us still at work. We'll be doing that too!

To your retirement.
A well-deserved reward for a job well done.

We don't know what we are going to do without you. But we're ready to find out.

To a man who always has his foot to the pedal, his shoulder to the wheel, and his nose to the grindstone. How he got any work done in that position I'll never know.

Merry met, and merry part, I drink to thee with all my heart.

May the hinges of our friendship never grow rusty.

Let's raise our glasses To the one that got away!

A toast to life without work,

The harder you work, the harder it is to surrender.

A toast to Woody Allen who said:
"I don't want to achieve immortality through my work,"
I want to achieve it through not dying.

SPORTS

Toasting is a part of the sporting life. It is fitting that a few should be suggested for whichever sport you follow.

Basketball
To basketball
Which is like the game of life
And can't be played alone!

* * * * *

Bungee jumping
You jumped off a bridge today
With just a cord around your feet.
If it had broken you would have gone splat
Where would the joy have been in that?

* * * * *

Cricket
A toast to the fine game of cricket
To bowlers, whether fast, spin or slow
And batsmen who stay in, never losing their wicket
Ah what a joy to watch the show!

* * * * *

Fishing
Here's to the fish that I may catch
So large that even I,
When talking of it afterwards
Will never need to lie!

* * * * *

Football
To football
What a wonderful sport!

The mark, the tackle, the goal!
The crowd going nuts and cheering.
What a buzz, what a thrill,
I'll keep going until
I'm just too old, blind and not hearing!

✻ ✻ ✻ ✻ ✻

Golf

Here's to the great game of golf
It makes you feel alive
But when you hit that ball all over the course
You'll need a cart with a four-wheel drive!

✻ ✻ ✻ ✻ ✻

Here's to your woods, here's to your irons,
Here's to your putter, too
May every shot you hit with them
Find the hole for you!

✻ ✻ ✻ ✻ ✻

Horse Racing

Let's toast the nags that ran today
We're hoarse from cheering them on!
And no matter what is said and done,
You often wish you'd backed … another one!

✻ ✻ ✻ ✻ ✻

Ice hockey

To the sport of ice hockey
Where part of the game is mental
And part is being mental.

✻ ✻ ✻ ✻ ✻

Sailing

To sailing
Where it's said there's no thrills when skies are clear and blue
And no skill in doing what others claim to do,
But there is some satisfaction which is mighty sweet to take
When you sail into a harbour that you never thought to make.

✫ ✫ ✫ ✫ ✫

Soccer

To the incredible game of soccer
Which can be played up and down the field for hours
And still the score reads "Nil—all"

✫ ✫ ✫ ✫ ✫

Ten pin bowling

To that cunning game of ten pins
You must make them all fall down.
But if you only hit a few
Your job's cut out to hit the rest,
And so and so and so.

✫ ✫ ✫ ✫ ✫

Tennis

Let's drink to tennis
A cynic's game where love means nothing
Even though it means everything in life.

✫ ✫ ✫ ✫ ✫

St Patrick's Day

Did you know the Chicago River is dyed Kelly green on St Patrick's Day? They rest of the year it's just brown. It's such a popular holiday, but sure why wouldn't it get lots of publicity? The people who sell the booze make a fortune! So toast this fun day.

> Today's the day to wear the green
> And take a nip of whiskey
> And drink and sing and kiss the girls
> And get a wee bit frisky!

* * * * *

> There's many an Irishman likes his drink
> He'd rather it was green than pink.
> You needn't worry, he's still able to think
> He could think you under the table!

* * * * *

> A drink to the Irish on St Paddy's Day
> Where all their wars are merry
> And all their songs are sad!

* * * * *

> A toast to the ghost of St Patrick
> Who drove the snakes from Ireland
> Could he do the same for us?

* * * * *

> Lift your glasses and have no fear
> It may be green but it's still good beer!

* * * * *

On this St Patrick's,
Surrounded by friends four score
Take that fella wearing "Kiss me, I'm Irish!" pin
And chuck him out the door!

* * * * *

A toast to the Irish
St Patrick and Mary Mac
To shamrocks and emerald isles
Green beer and great crack!

* * * * *

A toast on St Patrick's Day
There are many good reasons for drinking,
One has just entered my head.
If a man doesn't drink when he's living,
How in the hell can he drink when he's dead?

* * * * *

St Patrick we are grateful
You joined us from gay Paree
If you hadn't come over to the Emerald Isle
We'd have no good excuse for this fesitivit—ee.

* * * * *

To St Patrick's Day
The best excuse all year
To get totally stocious
And full of green beer.

* * * * *

Here's to Guinness, here's to stout
Drink up! Drink up! 'tis now your shout!

* * * * *

Let's drink to smiling Irish eyes
And the lilt of Irish laughter.
To shamrocks and leprechauns
Green beer and Guinness,
Have another pint on me
'tis Paddy's Day, my goo'ness!

✣ ✣ ✣ ✣ ✣

Ah let's drink to the best of saints
And his name is Saint Patrick.
Drove the snakes from Ireland did he
And has helped the brewery.
There's not a saint, I do think
Who could so turn a man to drink!

✣ ✣ ✣ ✣ ✣

To drink
Alcohol may be your worst enemy
But the Bible says, "Love your enemy!"
And the Irish are such a God fearing lot.

✣ ✣ ✣ ✣ ✣

STAG'S PARTY

Stag parties are intended to be the groom's last hoorah before he settles down to wedded bliss. His bachelor friends will of course tease him about this defection.

In practice, it is best to schedule bachelor parties several days prior to the wedding ceremony so that the groom and his party can recover.

What a great opportunity to seize the moment and toast...the groom-to-be, bachelorhood, friendship, women...

> Here's to being single...
> Drinking doubles...
> And seeing triple!

* * * * *

Here's to Life, Liberty and the Happiness of Pursuit!

* * * * *

> A toast to Oscar Wilde who said,
> "Men marry because they are tired;
> women because they're curious.
> Both are disappointed."

* * * * *

Here's to the pleasures and freedom of the single life...
May my memory now fail me!

* * * * *

> The men in college,
> The he-men and the wrecks,
> They do a lot of talking
> About drinking and about sex.

Now it's been observed,
In spite of what they boast of,
That between the drinking and women
Drinking is what they get the most of.

* * * * *

A book, a game, a fire, a friend
A beer that's always full.
Here's to the joys of a bachelor's life
A life that's never dull.

* * * * *

'tis better to have loved and lost
Than to get marry and be bossed.

* * * * *

Here's to giving up the bachelor's food categories,
FAST, FROZEN AND INSTANT!

* * * * *

Say it with flowers, say it with sweets,
Say it with kisses, say it with eats,
Say it with jewellery, say it with drink,
But whatever you do don't say it with ink.

* * * * *

It's a funny thing that when man don't have anything on earth to worry about
He goes off and gets married. — Robert Frost

* * * * *

A toast to a man called Mencken who wisely said:
"Bachelors know more about women than married men; if they didn't, they'd be married too."

* * * * *

A toast to the virtues of marriage,
I'm told marriage is popular because it combines the maximum of temptation with the maximum of opportunity.

✻ ✻ ✻ ✻ ✻

Let's toast the difference:
He who marries might be sorry,
but he who does not will be sorry.

✻ ✻ ✻ ✻ ✻

To men,
It's true that all men are born free and equal...
but some of them go and get MARRIED!

✻ ✻ ✻ ✻ ✻

Let's drink to 'before and after'
Before marriage a man yearns for the woman he loves; after marriage the 'y' becomes silent!

✻ ✻ ✻ ✻ ✻

To being heard,
If you want your wife to listen carefully to everything you say, try talking in your sleep.

✻ ✻ ✻ ✻ ✻

Team Won/Lost

Winning or losing usually involves a spot of drinking, be it celebrating or commisserating. So why not a toast, either way?

We won!

To Lombardi who said:
"Winning isn't everything, it's the only thing."

* * * * *

Winning isn't everything. But the *will to win* is.

* * * * *

Hip! Hip! Hooray!
We won today
Let's rejoice and raise our glasses
We didn't only beat their team
We really kicked their arses!

* * * * *

To the rush you get when you have won
It keeps you going for hours
Long after the setting sun
You go on celebrating!

* * * * *

A toast to our team who've won today
How sweet a thing to hear!
The crowd all going wild with glee,
Now you deserve free beer!

We Lost!

We lost again, we just can't win
Our team just has bad luck
Unless of course, it's all our fault
And we just really suck!

✳ ✳ ✳ ✳ ✳

It's not winning or losing it's how you play the game.
Interesting that you only hear this wisdom from losers!

✳ ✳ ✳ ✳ ✳

A toast to wise man Ingersoll who said
"The best test of courage is to bear defeat without losing heart."

✳ ✳ ✳ ✳ ✳

To keeping on keeping on
So we lost today, but that doesn't mean we've lost our nerve!
We need to get back out there next time
And try all over again!

✳ ✳ ✳ ✳ ✳

Who share in this defeat!
We'll live to fight another day
And victory will seem so sweet!

✳ ✳ ✳ ✳ ✳

A toast to never giving up,
Even though we went down today!
We're made of stronger stuff than most
And will go on trying till we win the day!

✳ ✳ ✳ ✳ ✳

Valentine's Day

A day for lovers or those who would like to be! A day for greeting cards, assignations, chocolates and gifts and confessing your love. The romance of the day is enhanced by making a romantic toast.

> To my Valentine
> I love you
> And more
> I love who I am
> when I'm with you.

* * * * *

> Because you are my true love
> Because you love me too
> My very greatest happiness
> Is spending time with you.

* * * * *

> Let's drink to Cupid the imp of love
> Whose aim went straight to the heart
> The moment I saw you I was lost
> Wanted to hold you and never part.

* * * * *

> Here's to the love I hold for you
> May it every day get stronger
> May it last as long as your love for me
> And not a moment longer!

* * * * *

> I drink to you my charming friend
> Hope that our love never ends.

* * * * *

Roses are red
Violets are blue
Have you any idea
How much I love you?

✻ ✻ ✻ ✻ ✻

Here's to the love of my life
My friend, my helper, my darling wife!

✻ ✻ ✻ ✻ ✻

Here's to my darling mate,
Thanks for the chocolates and the date!

✻ ✻ ✻ ✻ ✻

A toast to you, my darling,
And to St Valentine
Who's made me brave enough to ask,
"Would you…like another glass of wine?"

✻ ✻ ✻ ✻ ✻

To you a toast, My Valentine!
To your shining eyes when they look into mine.
I can't think of a place I'd rather be
Than sitting here with you close to me!

✻ ✻ ✻ ✻ ✻

To St Valentine, the cupid saint
Take pity on the meek
Who wait the whole year, day in day out
To finally get up and speak,
"I love you!" There I said it,
Your answer do I seek!

✻ ✻ ✻ ✻ ✻

WAKES AND REMEMBRANCES

A toast to absent friends… If you were the first to go, wouldn't you want to be remembered sometimes when your friends were gathered together? Make a toast to those who have died, whom you know are still with you in spirit.

> Oh here's to other meetings
> And merry greetings then
> And here's to those we've drunk with
> But never can again!

✻ ✻ ✻ ✻ ✻

> To our dear friend we miss you
> You livened up our days
> Each time we gather we drink to you
> And think of you always.

✻ ✻ ✻ ✻ ✻

> 'tis sad that you have parted
> But to us you're still right here.
> You live on in our memories
> The one we hold so dear.

✻ ✻ ✻ ✻ ✻

> To _____
> You live in hearts you've left behind
> Which means you never die!

✻ ✻ ✻ ✻ ✻

To our friend who was called away
A year ago on this very day.
We remember you well
And often tell
Of the times we shared, of the things you'd say.

※ ※ ※ ※ ※

It's been a few years since you've been gone
But you are remembered so fondly by everyone.

※ ※ ※ ※ ※

Dear friend, this drink's for you
We often miss you and wish you were here
Sitting with us, sharing a beer!

※ ※ ※ ※ ※

A toast to you, our missing friends!
We think of you each day
And even though you're absent,
In our hearts you'll always stay.

※ ※ ※ ※ ※

We drink to your fond memory
The times we shared together.
We miss you friend, we really do,
In stormy or pleasant weather!

※ ※ ※ ※ ※

To friends who can't be here with us,
Who would be if they could!
Sharing in the fun and laughter,
The bad times and the good.

※ ※ ※ ※ ※

WASSAIL! – THE DRINKING OCCASION

Wassail comes from Saxon,"was hail", meaning to greet or say goodbye to someone and it meant, "Be in good health". By the twelfth century it became the salutation you offered as a toast. Later on it came to be used for the drink in which the toast was offered, especially the spiced ale and mulled wine drunk on Christmas Eve or Twelfth Night. The apple tree was toasted in the hopes it would bear generous crops for the next year's cider.

> Then here's to the heartening wassail,
> Wherever good fellows are found;
> Be its master instead of its vassal,
> And order the glasses around. — Ogden Nash

※ ※ ※ ※ ※

> I drink to your health when I'm with you,
> I drink to your health when I'm alone,
> I drink to your health so often,
> I'm starting to worry about my own!

※ ※ ※ ※ ※

> Here's to wine!
> That lifts our spirits
> And drowns our sorrows
> And makes us worry less
> About our tomorrows!

※ ※ ※ ※ ※

> Drinking will make a man quaff,
> Quaffing will make a man sing,
> Singing will make a man laugh,
> And laughing long life doth bring. — Thomas D'Urfey

※ ※ ※ ※ ※

Here's to champagne, the drink divine
Which makes us forget all our troubles
It's made from ten dollars worth of wine
And twenty dollars worth of bubbles!

※ ※ ※ ※ ※

Here's to women's kisses,
and to whiskey, amber clear;
Not as sweet as a woman's kiss,
but a darn sight more sincere!

※ ※ ※ ※ ※

Let's toast the art of drinking
Of being of good cheer
Let's toast the wine and liquor
The whiskey and the beer.

※ ※ ※ ※ ※

Let's raise our glasses and drink to drinking
That stops a man from too much thinking!

※ ※ ※ ※ ※

Let every man take off his hat
And shout out to th'old apple tree
Old apple tree we wassail thee
And hoping thou will bear.

※ ※ ※ ※ ※

Oh God of wine deliver me
When half across life's stormy sea
From Snares and Sins of every sort
And bring me safely back to Port!

※ ※ ※ ※ ※

A little wine they often say
Is good for the health
And keeps cares away.

But drink too much
You'll rue the day.

* * * * *

Gift of Bacchus
The loving cup
It spilleth over
Can't get enough!

* * * * *

Gad made man, frail as a bubble,
God made love—love made trouble.
God made the vine
Then is it a sin
That man made wine
To drown trouble in?

* * * * *

There are three reasons we would drink:
A warm toast.
Good company.
A fine wine.
May you enjoy all three.

* * * * *

God in His goodness sent the grapes,
to cheer both great and small;
little fools will drink too much,
and great fools not at all.

* * * * *

Life, alas,
Is very dear.
Up with the glass,
Down with the beer!

* * * * *

Here's to wine which improves with age,
I like it more the older I get.

* * * * *

Who loves not women, wine, and song,
Remains a fool his whole life long.

* * * * *

To wine and women—may we always have a taste for both.

* * * * *

A toast to Lord Byron who said:
Let us have wine and women
mirth and laughter,
Sermons and soda-water the day after.

* * * * *

Here's to mine and here's to thine!
Now's the time to clink it!
Here's a flagon of old wine,
And here we are to drink it.

* * * * *

To temperance…in moderation.—Lem Motlow

* * * * *

Where there is plenty of wine,
sorrow and worry take wing.

* * * * *

Here's to the man who knows enough
To know he's better without the stuff;
Himself without, the wine within,
So come, me hearties, let's begin.

* * * * *

When wine enlivens the heart,
may friendship surround the table.

* * * * *

Here's Champagne to our real friends
and real pain to our sham friends.

✻ ✻ ✻ ✻ ✻

That the tap may be open when it rusts!

✻ ✻ ✻ ✻ ✻

My friends are the best friends
Loyal, willing and able.
Now let's get to drinking!
All glasses off the table!

✻ ✻ ✻ ✻ ✻

Here's to a long life and a merry one.
A quick death and an easy one.
A pretty girl and an honest one.
A cold pint—and another one!

✻ ✻ ✻ ✻ ✻

When money's tight and hard to get,
and your horse is also ran,
When all you have is a heap of debt,
a pint of plain is your only man.

✻ ✻ ✻ ✻ ✻

To beer!
In heaven there's no beer
That's why we drink ours here.

✻ ✻ ✻ ✻ ✻

For every wound, a balm.
For every sorrow, cheer.
For every storm, a calm.
For every thirst, a beer.

✻ ✻ ✻ ✻ ✻

Be one who drinks the finest of ales.
Every day without fail.
Even when you have drank enough,
Remember that ale is wonderful stuff.

※ ※ ※ ※ ※

Thirsty days hath September,
April, June and November;
All the rest are thirsty too
Except for him who hath home brew.

※ ※ ※ ※ ※

Who'd care to be a bee and sip
Sweet honey from the flower's lip
When he might be a fly and steer
Head first into a can of beer?

※ ※ ※ ※ ※

WEDDINGS

Weddings, more than any other of life's celebrations, are an occasion when at least a few toasts, if not entire speeches, are fully expected.

The classic wedding toasts are "Health and happiness!" and "May all your troubles be little ones!" However they have become old hat. You will find some fresher suggestions included.

The traditional order is the father of the bride, followed by the groom and lastly the best man, however there can be many additions and variations, and now it is quite common for women to toast at weddings.

TO THE BRIDE AND GROOM

Here's a toast to____and____. I believe love can last forever and grow stronger with time. This I wish for you today.

✻ ✻ ✻ ✻ ✻

Here's to the health of the happy pair;
May good fortune follow them everywhere.
And may each day of wedded bliss
Be as joyous as a day such as this.

✻ ✻ ✻ ✻ ✻

Please raise your toast to the bride and groom. May the love they feel for each other today become only a pale shadow of what is to come.

✻ ✻ ✻ ✻ ✻

A toast to the health of the bride
A toast to the health of the groom

A toast to the person the knot who tied
A toast to every guest in the room!

⁂ ⁂ ⁂ ⁂ ⁂

Life is so much better when shared, so it's a wonderful thing that you have found each other. May your life together be filled with loving, giving and caring. Here's to____ and____

⁂ ⁂ ⁂ ⁂ ⁂

To keep a marriage brimming with love in the loving cup—
When you are wrong, admit it and when you are right, shut up!

⁂ ⁂ ⁂ ⁂ ⁂

Here's to the groom and his lady
And to this wonderful wedding
Have a care for the drink and dancing
Or you won't have any puff for the bedding!

⁂ ⁂ ⁂ ⁂ ⁂

May you both live as long as you want,
And never want as long as you live.

⁂ ⁂ ⁂ ⁂ ⁂

Happy marriages begin when we marry the one we love, and they blossom when we love the one we married.

⁂ ⁂ ⁂ ⁂ ⁂

To Adam and Eve and the ideal marriage,
He didn't have to hear about all the men she could have married
And she didn't have to hear about how his mother cooked.

⁂ ⁂ ⁂ ⁂ ⁂

To the newlyweds.
May "for better or worse" be much better than worse.

⁂ ⁂ ⁂ ⁂ ⁂

Toast for Life's Occasions

May your troubles be less
And your blessings be more.
And nothing but happiness
Come through your door.

❈ ❈ ❈ ❈ ❈

May the roof above you never fall in, and may you both never fall out.

❈ ❈ ❈ ❈ ❈

Coming together is a beginning; keeping together is progress; working together is success.

❈ ❈ ❈ ❈ ❈

Here's to the bride all here you see,
Here's to the groom that she has wed
May all their troubles be light as bubbles
Or the feathers that make up their bed!

❈ ❈ ❈ ❈ ❈

Here's to the husband, and here's to his wife
May they remain lovers all of their life!

❈ ❈ ❈ ❈ ❈

May their joys be bright as the morning, and their sorrows just shadows that vanish in the sunshine of love.

❈ ❈ ❈ ❈ ❈

May you grow old on one pillow.

❈ ❈ ❈ ❈ ❈

The greatest of all arts is the art of living together.

❈ ❈ ❈ ❈ ❈

To the one we love—
when she is our toast we don't want anyone but her.

❈ ❈ ❈ ❈ ❈

Love doesn't make the world go round.
Love makes the ride worthwhile.

TO THE BRIDESMAIDS

Let's raise our glasses and toast our bridesmaids, who are not only lovely but have helped____(bride's name) to prepare for her special day. May they have health and happiness!

✣ ✣ ✣ ✣ ✣

A toast to the bridesmaids so fair
Who've increased our joy by being there
For the bride, groom, family and friends
Good fortune, good health, kind blessings!

TO THE GROOMSMEN

Let's toast the groomsmen, handsome and upstanding. Thank you for being such a help and support to _____ (groom's name) on this his special day.

✣ ✣ ✣ ✣ ✣

To the men who stood with the groom
God bless you each, from all in the room!

TO THE PARENTS

A toast to the parents of the bride and groom!
Bless you for making this day possible,
and for lending your support and love to the new pair!

✣ ✣ ✣ ✣ ✣

To both our families
May they grow close
Woven together by the love
Of these two.

GROOM TO HIS BRIDE

To my lovely wife ____.
You have made me a very happy man.
I plan to love you and support you
every day of our life together.

* * * * *

To my darling ____
Grow old with me,
The best is yet to be.

* * * * *

To my bride,
My love, my best friend,
Come away with me, let's start our life!

* * * * *

To my darling ....
Thank you for saying Yes,
I will spend the rest of my life
Making you happy you agreed
To be my wife.

* * * * *

To my wife. My bride and joy.

* * * * *

Come, come away with me!
The best is yet to be!
Let's drink a toast to this lovely woman
Who has made me the happiest man
By marrying me today!

BRIDE TO HER GROOM

Let's raise a glass and toast my handsome husband.
I am so lucky to have your love and caring.
I can't wait to begin our life together.

✻ ✻ ✻ ✻ ✻

To my dearest husband,
Never below you, never above you,
Always beside you!

✻ ✻ ✻ ✻ ✻

To the man by my side,
Who has made me his bride.
I love you with all my heart
Just as I loved you from the start!

✻ ✻ ✻ ✻ ✻

Winning the Lottery

You may well think it's farfetched to include a few toasts for this rare occasion. But just in case, and to be prepared, here are a few you might like to have in store, in case you ever got lucky or someone else you know does.

> Congratulations!
> The jackpot you've hit.
> Remember we were your friends
> Before you got rich!

> What a lucky stroke it is for you
> Your numbers have come in.
> May your luck rub off on us
> Then the rest of us could win!

> Congratulations to you and yours
> Couldn't wish this bit of fortune on a more deserving family!

> Let's raise our glasses and drink a toast
> To this man who is our gracious host.
> Good luck on your winnings
> And to new beginnings!